50 Traditional Indian Curries for Home

By: Kelly Johnson

Table of Contents

- Butter Chicken (Murgh Makhani)
- Chicken Tikka Masala
- Rogan Josh
- Chicken Korma
- Palak Paneer
- Dal Makhani
- Chana Masala
- Aloo Gobi
- Baingan Bharta
- Goan Fish Curry
- Prawn Malai Curry
- Mutton Keema Curry
- Shahi Paneer
- Malabar Chicken Curry
- Bhindi Masala
- Dum Aloo
- Kadai Paneer
- Chettinad Chicken Curry
- Lamb Vindaloo
- Methi Malai Murg
- Bengali Mustard Fish Curry
- Hyderabadi Mirchi Ka Salan
- Mushroom Masala
- Punjabi Kadhi Pakora
- Kerala Coconut Chicken Curry
- Egg Curry (Anda Curry)
- Rajasthani Laal Maas
- Dal Tadka
- Mangalorean Fish Curry
- Parsi Dhansak
- Kashmiri Yakhni
- Paneer Butter Masala
- Gujarati Undhiyu
- Sarson Da Saag
- Kolhapuri Chicken Curry

- Masoor Dal Curry
- Sindhi Kadhi
- Jackfruit (Kathal) Curry
- Mutton Curry (Railway Style)
- Mysore Mutton Curry
- Moong Dal Curry
- Soya Chaap Masala
- Chicken Rezala
- Gatte Ki Sabzi
- Tomato Curry (Tamatar Ka Salan)
- Drumstick Curry
- Black Chana Curry
- Achari Chicken
- Karela (Bitter Gourd) Curry
- Sambar

Butter Chicken (Murgh Makhani)

Ingredients

For the Chicken Marinade

- 500g (1 lb) boneless chicken thighs or breast, cut into bite-sized pieces
- ½ cup plain yogurt
- 1 tbsp lemon juice
- 1 tsp turmeric powder
- 1 tsp chili powder (adjust to taste)
- 1 tsp garam masala
- 1 tsp ground cumin
- 1 tsp ground coriander
- ½ tsp salt
- 2 cloves garlic, minced
- 1-inch ginger, grated

For the Sauce

- 2 tbsp butter
- 1 tbsp oil
- 1 onion, finely chopped
- 2 cloves garlic, minced
- 1-inch ginger, grated
- 1 tsp cumin
- 1 tsp garam masala
- 1 tsp ground coriander
- 1 tsp chili powder (adjust to taste)
- ½ tsp turmeric
- 1 cup tomato purée (or canned crushed tomatoes)
- ½ cup heavy cream (or coconut cream for a dairy-free option)
- ½ tsp sugar (optional)
- Salt to taste
- Fresh cilantro (for garnish)

Instructions

1. Marinate the Chicken

1. In a bowl, mix yogurt, lemon juice, turmeric, chili powder, garam masala, cumin, coriander, salt, garlic, and ginger.
2. Add the chicken pieces, coat well, cover, and refrigerate for at least **1 hour** (overnight for best flavor).

2. Cook the Chicken

1. Heat a pan or grill over medium-high heat. Add a little oil and cook the marinated chicken pieces until slightly charred and cooked through (about **5-7 minutes per side**). Set aside.

3. Make the Sauce

1. In the same pan, melt butter and add a little oil. Sauté onions until soft and golden.
2. Add garlic, ginger, cumin, garam masala, coriander, chili powder, and turmeric. Stir for **30 seconds** until fragrant.
3. Pour in the tomato purée and cook for **10 minutes**, stirring occasionally.
4. Add the heavy cream, sugar (if using), and salt to taste. Simmer for **5 minutes** until thickened.

4. Combine & Serve

1. Add the cooked chicken back into the sauce and simmer for **5 minutes** to absorb flavors.
2. Garnish with fresh cilantro and serve hot with naan or basmati rice.

Chicken Tikka Masala

Ingredients

For the Chicken Marinade:

- 500g (1 lb) boneless chicken thighs or breast, cut into chunks
- ½ cup plain yogurt
- 1 tbsp lemon juice
- 1 tsp turmeric
- 1 tsp cumin
- 1 tsp garam masala
- 1 tsp chili powder
- ½ tsp salt
- 2 cloves garlic, minced
- 1-inch ginger, grated

For the Sauce:

- 2 tbsp butter or oil
- 1 onion, finely chopped
- 2 cloves garlic, minced
- 1-inch ginger, grated
- 1 tsp cumin
- 1 tsp garam masala
- 1 tsp coriander
- 1 tsp chili powder
- ½ tsp turmeric
- 1 cup tomato purée
- ½ cup heavy cream
- Salt to taste
- Fresh cilantro for garnish

Instructions

1. **Marinate the chicken:** Mix yogurt, lemon juice, and spices. Coat chicken and refrigerate for 1 hour.
2. **Cook the chicken:** Grill or pan-fry until lightly charred. Set aside.
3. **Prepare the sauce:** Sauté onions in butter until golden, then add garlic, ginger, and spices. Stir in tomato purée and simmer for 10 minutes.

4. **Combine & serve:** Add chicken to the sauce, pour in cream, and simmer for 5 minutes. Garnish with cilantro. Serve with rice or naan.

Rogan Josh

Ingredients

- 500g (1 lb) lamb or chicken, cubed
- 2 tbsp oil or ghee
- 1 onion, finely chopped
- 2 cloves garlic, minced
- 1-inch ginger, grated
- 1 tsp cumin
- 1 tsp garam masala
- 1 tsp ground coriander
- 1 tsp paprika
- 1 tsp chili powder (adjust to taste)
- ½ tsp turmeric
- 1 cup tomato purée
- ½ cup yogurt
- Salt to taste
- Fresh cilantro for garnish

Instructions

1. **Brown the meat:** Heat oil in a pan and sear the meat until golden. Remove and set aside.
2. **Make the base:** Sauté onions until soft, then add garlic, ginger, and spices. Cook for 1 minute.
3. **Simmer the curry:** Add tomato purée, yogurt, and browned meat. Cover and cook on low heat for 40–50 minutes (until meat is tender).
4. **Serve:** Garnish with cilantro and serve with basmati rice or naan.

Chicken Korma

Ingredients

- 500g (1 lb) boneless chicken, cut into pieces
- ½ cup plain yogurt
- 2 tbsp oil or ghee
- 1 onion, finely chopped
- 2 cloves garlic, minced
- 1-inch ginger, grated
- 1 tsp cumin
- 1 tsp ground coriander
- 1 tsp garam masala
- ½ tsp turmeric
- 1 tsp cardamom powder
- ½ cup coconut milk or heavy cream
- ¼ cup ground almonds (optional)
- Salt to taste
- Fresh cilantro for garnish

Instructions

1. **Marinate the chicken:** Mix yogurt with half of the spices. Coat the chicken and let it marinate for 1 hour.
2. **Cook the base:** Heat oil, sauté onions until golden, then add garlic, ginger, and remaining spices.
3. **Simmer the curry:** Add chicken and cook for 10 minutes. Pour in coconut milk (or cream) and almonds. Simmer for 10 minutes until thickened.
4. **Serve:** Garnish with cilantro and serve with naan or rice.

Palak Paneer

Ingredients

- 250g paneer, cubed
- 2 cups spinach, blanched and puréed
- 1 onion, finely chopped
- 2 cloves garlic, minced
- 1-inch ginger, grated
- 1 green chili, chopped
- ½ tsp cumin
- ½ tsp garam masala
- ½ tsp turmeric
- ½ cup heavy cream (optional)
- 2 tbsp oil or ghee
- Salt to taste

Instructions

1. Heat oil in a pan, sauté onions until golden. Add garlic, ginger, and chili.
2. Stir in cumin, garam masala, turmeric, and spinach purée. Cook for 5 minutes.
3. Add paneer, mix well, and simmer for another 5 minutes. Stir in cream if using.
4. Serve hot with roti or rice.

Dal Makhani

Ingredients

- 1 cup whole black lentils (urad dal)
- ¼ cup kidney beans
- 1 onion, finely chopped
- 2 tomatoes, puréed
- 2 cloves garlic, minced
- 1-inch ginger, grated
- ½ tsp cumin
- 1 tsp garam masala
- ½ tsp chili powder
- ½ cup heavy cream
- 2 tbsp butter
- Salt to taste

Instructions

1. Soak lentils and kidney beans overnight, then boil until soft.
2. In a pan, heat butter and sauté onions. Add garlic, ginger, and spices.
3. Stir in tomatoes and cook for 10 minutes. Add cooked lentils and simmer for 20 minutes.
4. Stir in cream and cook for another 5 minutes. Serve with naan or rice.

Chana Masala

Ingredients

- 1 cup chickpeas, soaked overnight and boiled
- 1 onion, finely chopped
- 2 tomatoes, puréed
- 2 cloves garlic, minced
- 1-inch ginger, grated
- 1 tsp cumin
- 1 tsp coriander powder
- 1 tsp garam masala
- ½ tsp chili powder
- ½ tsp turmeric
- 2 tbsp oil
- Salt to taste

Instructions

1. Heat oil in a pan, sauté onions until golden. Add garlic, ginger, and spices.
2. Stir in tomatoes and cook for 10 minutes. Add chickpeas and simmer for 10 minutes.
3. Garnish with cilantro and serve with rice or roti.

Aloo Gobi

Ingredients

- 2 potatoes, diced
- 1 small cauliflower, cut into florets
- 1 onion, finely chopped
- 2 tomatoes, chopped
- 2 cloves garlic, minced
- 1-inch ginger, grated
- 1 tsp cumin
- 1 tsp coriander powder
- ½ tsp turmeric
- ½ tsp chili powder
- 2 tbsp oil
- Salt to taste

Instructions

1. Heat oil, add cumin, then sauté onions until golden.
2. Add garlic, ginger, and spices. Stir in potatoes and cauliflower.
3. Add tomatoes, cover, and cook for 15 minutes.
4. Serve hot with roti or paratha.

Baingan Bharta

Ingredients

- 1 large eggplant
- 1 onion, finely chopped
- 2 tomatoes, chopped
- 2 cloves garlic, minced
- 1-inch ginger, grated
- 1 tsp cumin
- ½ tsp garam masala
- ½ tsp chili powder
- 2 tbsp oil
- Salt to taste

Instructions

1. Roast eggplant over an open flame or in the oven until soft. Peel and mash.
2. Heat oil, sauté onions, then add garlic, ginger, and spices.
3. Stir in tomatoes and cook for 5 minutes. Add mashed eggplant and cook for 10 minutes.
4. Garnish with cilantro and serve with roti.

Goan Fish Curry

Ingredients

- 500g firm white fish, cut into pieces
- 1 onion, finely chopped
- 2 tomatoes, puréed
- 1 cup coconut milk
- 2 cloves garlic, minced
- 1-inch ginger, grated
- 1 tsp turmeric
- 1 tsp coriander powder
- 1 tsp garam masala
- 1 tsp red chili powder
- 2 tbsp oil
- Salt to taste

Instructions

1. Heat oil in a pan, sauté onions until golden. Add garlic, ginger, and spices.
2. Stir in tomatoes and cook for 5 minutes. Add coconut milk and bring to a simmer.
3. Add fish and cook for 10 minutes until tender.
4. Serve hot with steamed rice.

Prawn Malai Curry

Ingredients

- 500g prawns, cleaned
- 1 onion, finely chopped
- 1 cup coconut milk
- 2 cloves garlic, minced
- 1-inch ginger, grated
- 1 tsp turmeric
- 1 tsp garam masala
- ½ tsp chili powder
- 2 tbsp mustard oil
- Salt to taste

Instructions

1. Heat oil, add onions and sauté until golden. Add garlic, ginger, and spices.
2. Pour in coconut milk and bring to a simmer.
3. Add prawns and cook for 5 minutes.
4. Serve with basmati rice.

Mutton Keema Curry

Ingredients

- 500g minced mutton
- 1 onion, finely chopped
- 2 tomatoes, chopped
- 2 cloves garlic, minced
- 1-inch ginger, grated
- 1 tsp cumin
- 1 tsp garam masala
- 1 tsp coriander powder
- ½ tsp turmeric
- ½ tsp chili powder
- 2 tbsp oil
- Salt to taste

Instructions

1. Heat oil in a pan, sauté onions until golden. Add garlic, ginger, and spices.
2. Stir in tomatoes and cook for 5 minutes. Add minced mutton and cook for 15 minutes.
3. Garnish with cilantro and serve with roti or rice.

Shahi Paneer

Ingredients:

- 250g paneer, cubed
- 1 onion, finely chopped
- 2 tomatoes, puréed
- ¼ cup cashew paste
- ½ cup heavy cream
- 2 cloves garlic, minced
- 1-inch ginger, grated
- 1 tsp cumin
- 1 tsp garam masala
- ½ tsp turmeric
- ½ tsp chili powder
- 2 tbsp ghee or butter
- Salt to taste

Instructions:

1. Heat ghee, sauté onions, then add garlic and ginger.
2. Stir in cumin, garam masala, turmeric, and chili powder.
3. Add tomatoes and cashew paste, cook for 10 minutes.
4. Stir in cream and paneer, simmer for 5 minutes.
5. Serve hot with naan or rice.

Malabar Chicken Curry

Ingredients:

- 500g chicken, cut into pieces
- 1 onion, finely chopped
- 2 tomatoes, chopped
- 1 cup coconut milk
- 2 cloves garlic, minced
- 1-inch ginger, grated
- 1 tsp fennel seeds
- 1 tsp garam masala
- ½ tsp turmeric
- 1 tsp red chili powder
- 2 tbsp coconut oil
- Salt to taste

Instructions:

1. Heat oil, sauté onions, then add garlic, ginger, and spices.
2. Stir in tomatoes, cook for 5 minutes.
3. Add chicken and coconut milk, simmer for 20 minutes.
4. Serve hot with appam or rice.

Bhindi Masala

Ingredients:

- 250g okra (bhindi), chopped
- 1 onion, sliced
- 2 tomatoes, chopped
- 2 cloves garlic, minced
- 1-inch ginger, grated
- 1 tsp cumin
- 1 tsp coriander powder
- ½ tsp turmeric
- ½ tsp chili powder
- 2 tbsp oil
- Salt to taste

Instructions:

1. Heat oil, sauté okra until slightly crispy. Remove and set aside.
2. In the same pan, sauté onions, then add garlic, ginger, and spices.
3. Stir in tomatoes, cook for 5 minutes, then add okra back.
4. Cook for another 5 minutes and serve with roti.

Dum Aloo

Ingredients:

- 500g baby potatoes, boiled and peeled
- 1 onion, finely chopped
- 2 tomatoes, puréed
- ¼ cup yogurt
- 2 cloves garlic, minced
- 1-inch ginger, grated
- 1 tsp cumin
- 1 tsp garam masala
- ½ tsp turmeric
- ½ tsp chili powder
- 2 tbsp oil
- Salt to taste

Instructions:

1. Heat oil, fry potatoes until golden. Remove and set aside.
2. Sauté onions, then add garlic, ginger, and spices.
3. Stir in tomatoes and yogurt, cook for 5 minutes.
4. Add potatoes and simmer for 10 minutes. Serve with naan.

Kadai Paneer

Ingredients:

- 250g paneer, cubed
- 1 onion, sliced
- 1 green bell pepper, chopped
- 2 tomatoes, chopped
- 2 cloves garlic, minced
- 1-inch ginger, grated
- 1 tsp cumin
- 1 tsp garam masala
- ½ tsp turmeric
- 1 tsp red chili powder
- 2 tbsp oil
- Salt to taste

Instructions:

1. Heat oil, sauté onions and bell pepper until slightly soft. Remove and set aside.
2. In the same pan, sauté garlic, ginger, and spices.
3. Add tomatoes, cook for 5 minutes. Stir in paneer and cooked veggies.
4. Simmer for 5 minutes and serve hot with roti.

Chettinad Chicken Curry

Ingredients:

- 500g chicken, cut into pieces
- 1 onion, finely chopped
- 2 tomatoes, chopped
- 1 tsp fennel seeds
- 1 tsp black pepper
- 1 tsp coriander powder
- ½ tsp turmeric
- 1 tsp red chili powder
- 1 cup coconut milk
- 2 cloves garlic, minced
- 1-inch ginger, grated
- 2 tbsp oil
- Salt to taste

Instructions:

1. Heat oil, sauté onions, then add garlic, ginger, and spices.
2. Stir in tomatoes and cook for 5 minutes.
3. Add chicken and coconut milk, simmer for 20 minutes.
4. Serve hot with dosa or rice.

Lamb Vindaloo

Ingredients:

- 500g lamb, cubed
- 1 onion, finely chopped
- 2 tomatoes, chopped
- 2 cloves garlic, minced
- 1-inch ginger, grated
- 1 tbsp vinegar
- 1 tsp cumin
- 1 tsp garam masala
- ½ tsp turmeric
- 1 tsp red chili powder
- 2 tbsp oil
- Salt to taste

Instructions:

1. Marinate lamb with vinegar, garlic, and spices for 1 hour.
2. Heat oil, sauté onions, then add tomatoes and marinated lamb.
3. Cook for 40–50 minutes until tender.
4. Serve hot with rice or naan.

Methi Malai Murg

Ingredients:

- 500g chicken, cut into pieces
- 1 onion, finely chopped
- 2 tomatoes, chopped
- ¼ cup fresh fenugreek leaves (methi)
- ½ cup heavy cream
- 2 cloves garlic, minced
- 1-inch ginger, grated
- 1 tsp cumin
- 1 tsp garam masala
- ½ tsp turmeric
- 1 tsp coriander powder
- 2 tbsp oil
- Salt to taste

Instructions:

1. Heat oil, sauté onions, then add garlic, ginger, and spices.
2. Stir in tomatoes and fenugreek leaves, cook for 5 minutes.
3. Add chicken and cook for 15 minutes, then stir in cream.
4. Simmer for another 5 minutes and serve hot.

Bengali Mustard Fish Curry

Ingredients:

- 500g fish fillets (rohu or pomfret)
- 1 onion, finely chopped
- 2 tomatoes, chopped
- 1 tbsp mustard paste
- 1 cup coconut milk
- 2 cloves garlic, minced
- 1-inch ginger, grated
- ½ tsp turmeric
- 1 tsp mustard seeds
- 2 tbsp mustard oil
- Salt to taste

Instructions:

1. Heat mustard oil, fry fish until golden. Remove and set aside.
2. In the same oil, sauté mustard seeds, then add onions, garlic, and ginger.
3. Stir in tomatoes, mustard paste, and turmeric. Cook for 5 minutes.
4. Pour in coconut milk, add fish, and simmer for 10 minutes.
5. Serve hot with steamed rice.

Hyderabadi Mirchi Ka Salan

Ingredients:

- 6-8 large green chilies (de-seeded)
- 1 onion, finely chopped
- 2 tbsp peanuts
- 1 tbsp sesame seeds
- 1 tbsp coconut, grated
- 2 cloves garlic, minced
- 1-inch ginger, grated
- 1 tsp mustard seeds
- ½ tsp turmeric
- 1 tsp cumin
- 1 tsp coriander powder
- ½ tsp red chili powder
- 1 cup tamarind water
- 2 tbsp oil
- Salt to taste

Instructions:

1. Lightly fry the chilies and set aside.
2. Dry roast peanuts, sesame, and coconut, then grind into a paste.
3. Heat oil, add mustard seeds, then sauté onions, garlic, and ginger.
4. Add ground paste, spices, and tamarind water. Cook for 10 minutes.
5. Add fried chilies and simmer for 5 minutes. Serve with biryani.

Mushroom Masala

Ingredients:

- 250g mushrooms, sliced
- 1 onion, finely chopped
- 2 tomatoes, chopped
- 2 cloves garlic, minced
- 1-inch ginger, grated
- 1 tsp cumin
- 1 tsp garam masala
- ½ tsp turmeric
- 1 tsp coriander powder
- ½ cup coconut milk or cream
- 2 tbsp oil
- Salt to taste

Instructions:

1. Heat oil, sauté onions until golden. Add garlic, ginger, and spices.
2. Stir in tomatoes and cook for 5 minutes.
3. Add mushrooms, cook for 10 minutes. Pour in coconut milk.
4. Simmer for 5 minutes and serve with rice.

Punjabi Kadhi Pakora

Ingredients:

For Pakoras:

- 1 cup gram flour (besan)
- ½ tsp turmeric
- ½ tsp red chili powder
- ½ tsp carom seeds (ajwain)
- Water as needed
- Salt to taste
- Oil for frying

For Kadhi:

- 1 cup yogurt
- 2 tbsp gram flour
- 1 tsp mustard seeds
- ½ tsp cumin
- ½ tsp turmeric
- 1 tsp red chili powder
- 2 cups water
- 1 onion, chopped
- 2 cloves garlic, minced
- 1-inch ginger, grated
- 2 tbsp oil
- Salt to taste

Instructions:

1. Mix pakora ingredients, make a thick batter, and deep-fry small fritters.
2. Heat oil, temper mustard and cumin seeds, then sauté onions, garlic, and ginger.
3. Whisk yogurt with gram flour, turmeric, and chili powder.
4. Pour into the pan with water, simmer for 15 minutes.
5. Add pakoras and cook for 5 minutes. Serve hot.

Kerala Coconut Chicken Curry

Ingredients:

- 500g chicken, cut into pieces
- 1 onion, finely chopped
- 2 tomatoes, chopped
- 1 cup coconut milk
- 2 cloves garlic, minced
- 1-inch ginger, grated
- 1 tsp fennel seeds
- 1 tsp coriander powder
- ½ tsp turmeric
- 1 tsp red chili powder
- 2 tbsp coconut oil
- Salt to taste

Instructions:

1. Heat oil, sauté onions, then add garlic, ginger, and spices.
2. Stir in tomatoes, cook for 5 minutes.
3. Add chicken and coconut milk, simmer for 20 minutes.
4. Serve hot with Kerala parotta.

Egg Curry (Anda Curry)

Ingredients:

- 4 boiled eggs, slit
- 1 onion, finely chopped
- 2 tomatoes, chopped
- 2 cloves garlic, minced
- 1-inch ginger, grated
- 1 tsp cumin
- 1 tsp garam masala
- ½ tsp turmeric
- 1 tsp red chili powder
- 2 tbsp oil
- Salt to taste

Instructions:

1. Heat oil, sauté onions, garlic, and ginger.
2. Add spices, stir in tomatoes, and cook for 10 minutes.
3. Add eggs, simmer for 5 minutes.
4. Serve with rice or chapati.

Rajasthani Laal Maas

Ingredients:

- 500g mutton, cut into pieces
- 3 dried red chilies
- 1 onion, finely chopped
- 2 cloves garlic, minced
- 1-inch ginger, grated
- 1 tsp cumin
- 1 tsp garam masala
- ½ tsp turmeric
- 1 tsp coriander powder
- ½ cup yogurt
- 2 tbsp mustard oil
- Salt to taste

Instructions:

1. Heat oil, sauté onions, then add garlic, ginger, and spices.
2. Stir in yogurt, mix well, then add mutton.
3. Cook on low heat for 40-50 minutes until tender.
4. Serve with roti or rice.

Dal Tadka

Ingredients:

- 1 cup toor dal (yellow lentils)
- 1 onion, chopped
- 2 tomatoes, chopped
- 2 cloves garlic, minced
- 1-inch ginger, grated
- 1 tsp cumin
- ½ tsp turmeric
- 1 tsp red chili powder
- 2 tbsp ghee
- Salt to taste

Instructions:

1. Cook dal with turmeric and salt.
2. Heat ghee, sauté cumin, onions, garlic, and ginger.
3. Add tomatoes, cook for 5 minutes, then mix with dal.
4. Serve with rice.

Mangalorean Fish Curry

Ingredients:

- 500g fish fillets
- 1 onion, chopped
- 2 tomatoes, chopped
- 1 cup coconut milk
- 2 cloves garlic, minced
- 1-inch ginger, grated
- 1 tsp mustard seeds
- 1 tsp coriander powder
- ½ tsp turmeric
- 1 tsp red chili powder
- 2 tbsp coconut oil
- Salt to taste

Instructions:

1. Heat oil, sauté mustard seeds, onions, garlic, and ginger.
2. Stir in tomatoes and spices, cook for 5 minutes.
3. Add coconut milk and fish, simmer for 10 minutes.
4. Serve with rice.

Parsi Dhansak

Ingredients:

- 500g lamb or chicken
- 1 cup mixed lentils (toor, moong, chana)
- 1 onion, chopped
- 2 tomatoes, chopped
- 2 cloves garlic, minced
- 1-inch ginger, grated
- 1 tsp cumin
- 1 tsp garam masala
- ½ tsp turmeric
- 1 tsp red chili powder
- 2 tbsp oil
- Salt to taste

Instructions:

1. Cook lentils with turmeric and salt.
2. Heat oil, sauté onions, garlic, and ginger.
3. Stir in tomatoes and spices, add meat, and cook for 40 minutes.
4. Mix in lentils and simmer for 10 minutes.
5. Serve with brown rice.

Kashmiri Yakhni

Ingredients:

- 500g lamb, cut into pieces
- 1 cup yogurt
- 2 cloves garlic, minced
- 1-inch ginger, grated
- 1 tsp fennel powder
- 1 tsp cumin
- ½ tsp turmeric
- 2 tbsp ghee
- Salt to taste

Instructions:

1. Heat ghee, sauté garlic, ginger, and spices.
2. Add lamb and cook for 40 minutes.
3. Stir in yogurt and simmer for 10 minutes.
4. Serve with rice.

Paneer Butter Masala

Ingredients:

- 250g paneer, cubed
- 1 onion, finely chopped
- 2 tomatoes, puréed
- 2 tbsp butter
- 1 tsp garam masala
- ½ tsp turmeric
- 1 tsp red chili powder
- ½ cup heavy cream
- Salt to taste

Instructions:

1. Heat butter, sauté onions, add tomatoes and spices.
2. Cook for 10 minutes, then add paneer and cream.
3. Simmer for 5 minutes and serve with naan.

Gujarati Undhiyu

Ingredients:

- 2 cups mixed vegetables (eggplant, potatoes, yam, green beans, carrots, and peas)
- 250g small potatoes, peeled
- 200g purple yam, chopped
- 1 cup purple brinjal (eggplant), chopped
- 1 cup green beans, chopped
- 2 tbsp sesame seeds
- 2 tbsp peanuts
- 2 tbsp coconut, grated
- 2 tbsp ginger-garlic paste
- 1 tsp cumin seeds
- 1 tsp mustard seeds
- 1 tsp turmeric
- 1 tsp garam masala
- 1 tbsp jaggery
- 2 tbsp tamarind pulp
- 2 tbsp oil
- Salt to taste

Instructions:

1. Heat oil, sauté cumin, mustard seeds, and ginger-garlic paste.
2. Add all the vegetables and cook for 5 minutes.
3. Stir in sesame seeds, peanuts, coconut, jaggery, and tamarind.
4. Cover and cook on low heat for 30-40 minutes, stirring occasionally.
5. Serve with puris or chapati.

Sarson Da Saag

Ingredients:

- 2 cups mustard leaves (sarson), chopped
- 1 cup spinach leaves (palak), chopped
- 1 onion, finely chopped
- 2 tomatoes, chopped
- 2 cloves garlic, minced
- 1-inch ginger, grated
- 1 tsp cumin seeds
- 1 tsp red chili powder
- ½ tsp turmeric powder
- 2 tbsp ghee
- Salt to taste

Instructions:

1. Boil mustard and spinach leaves until soft, then purée them.
2. Heat ghee, sauté cumin seeds, onions, garlic, and ginger.
3. Add tomatoes and cook for 5 minutes.
4. Stir in the puréed leaves, red chili powder, turmeric, and salt.
5. Simmer for 15 minutes, and serve with makki di roti.

Kolhapuri Chicken Curry

Ingredients:

- 500g chicken, cut into pieces
- 1 onion, finely chopped
- 2 tomatoes, chopped
- 2 cloves garlic, minced
- 1-inch ginger, grated
- 2 tsp Kolhapuri masala (or homemade Kolhapuri spice mix)
- 1 tsp cumin
- 1 tsp coriander powder
- 1 tsp garam masala
- ½ tsp turmeric
- 1 tbsp tamarind pulp
- 2 tbsp oil
- Salt to taste

Instructions:

1. Heat oil, sauté onions, garlic, and ginger.
2. Stir in spices and cook for 1-2 minutes.
3. Add tomatoes, cook for 5 minutes, then add chicken.
4. Add tamarind pulp, cover, and cook for 20 minutes until chicken is tender.
5. Serve with chapati or rice.

Masoor Dal Curry

Ingredients:

- 1 cup masoor dal (red lentils)
- 1 onion, chopped
- 2 tomatoes, chopped
- 2 cloves garlic, minced
- 1-inch ginger, grated
- 1 tsp cumin seeds
- ½ tsp turmeric
- 1 tsp garam masala
- 1 tsp red chili powder
- 2 tbsp oil
- Salt to taste

Instructions:

1. Cook dal with turmeric and salt until soft.
2. Heat oil, sauté cumin seeds, onions, garlic, and ginger.
3. Add tomatoes and cook for 5 minutes.
4. Stir in the cooked dal, red chili powder, and garam masala.
5. Simmer for 10 minutes, and serve with rice.

Sindhi Kadhi

Ingredients:

- 1 cup gram flour (besan)
- 1 onion, chopped
- 2 tomatoes, chopped
- 1 carrot, sliced
- 1 potato, cubed
- ½ cup drumsticks (vegetable)
- 1 tsp cumin seeds
- 1 tsp turmeric
- 1 tsp red chili powder
- 1 tbsp tamarind pulp
- 2 tbsp oil
- Salt to taste

Instructions:

1. Heat oil, sauté cumin seeds and onions.
2. Stir in gram flour and roast until lightly golden.
3. Add vegetables, tomatoes, and cook for 5 minutes.
4. Add turmeric, red chili powder, tamarind, and water, simmer for 15 minutes.
5. Serve with steamed rice.

Jackfruit (Kathal) Curry

Ingredients:

- 500g raw jackfruit, peeled and chopped
- 1 onion, finely chopped
- 2 tomatoes, chopped
- 2 cloves garlic, minced
- 1-inch ginger, grated
- 1 tsp cumin seeds
- 1 tsp coriander powder
- ½ tsp turmeric
- 1 tsp garam masala
- 2 tbsp oil
- Salt to taste

Instructions:

1. Heat oil, sauté cumin seeds, onions, garlic, and ginger.
2. Add tomatoes, cook for 5 minutes.
3. Add jackfruit, spices, and cook for 15 minutes.
4. Simmer until jackfruit is tender and serve with rice or roti.

Mutton Curry (Railway Style)

Ingredients:

- 500g mutton, cut into pieces
- 1 onion, finely chopped
- 2 tomatoes, chopped
- 2 cloves garlic, minced
- 1-inch ginger, grated
- 1 tsp cumin
- 1 tsp garam masala
- 1 tsp coriander powder
- ½ tsp turmeric
- 1 tbsp yogurt
- 2 tbsp oil
- Salt to taste

Instructions:

1. Heat oil, sauté onions, garlic, and ginger.
2. Stir in tomatoes, spices, and cook for 5 minutes.
3. Add mutton, cook until browned, then add yogurt.
4. Cook on low heat for 40 minutes.
5. Serve with chapati or rice.

Mysore Mutton Curry

Ingredients:

- 500g mutton, cut into pieces
- 1 onion, finely chopped
- 2 tomatoes, chopped
- 1 tsp cumin seeds
- 1 tsp coriander powder
- ½ tsp turmeric
- 1 tsp red chili powder
- 2 tbsp ginger-garlic paste
- 2 tbsp oil
- Salt to taste

Instructions:

1. Heat oil, sauté cumin seeds, onions, and ginger-garlic paste.
2. Add tomatoes, spices, and cook for 5 minutes.
3. Add mutton, cook until browned, and then simmer for 30 minutes.
4. Serve with rice or chapati.

Moong Dal Curry

Ingredients:

- 1 cup moong dal (yellow lentils)
- 1 onion, chopped
- 2 tomatoes, chopped
- 2 cloves garlic, minced
- 1-inch ginger, grated
- 1 tsp cumin seeds
- ½ tsp turmeric
- 1 tsp coriander powder
- 1 tsp garam masala
- 2 tbsp oil
- Salt to taste

Instructions:

1. Cook moong dal with turmeric and salt until soft.
2. Heat oil, sauté cumin seeds, onions, garlic, and ginger.
3. Add tomatoes and cook for 5 minutes.
4. Stir in the cooked dal, coriander powder, and garam masala.
5. Simmer for 10 minutes, and serve with rice or roti.

Soya Chaap Masala

Ingredients:

- 500g soya chaap (vegetarian meat substitute)
- 1 onion, finely chopped
- 2 tomatoes, chopped
- 2 tbsp ginger-garlic paste
- 1 tsp cumin seeds
- 1 tsp coriander powder
- 1 tsp garam masala
- ½ tsp turmeric
- 1 tsp red chili powder
- 2 tbsp yogurt
- 2 tbsp oil
- Fresh cilantro for garnish
- Salt to taste

Instructions:

1. Heat oil, sauté cumin seeds and onions until golden.
2. Add ginger-garlic paste, tomatoes, and cook for 5 minutes.
3. Stir in spices, then add yogurt and cook until the oil separates.
4. Add soya chaap pieces, mix well, and cook for 10 minutes.
5. Garnish with cilantro and serve with naan or rice.

Chicken Rezala

Ingredients:

- 500g chicken, cut into pieces
- 1 onion, finely chopped
- 2 tomatoes, chopped
- 2 cloves garlic, minced
- 1-inch ginger, grated
- 2 tbsp yogurt
- 1 tsp cumin
- 1 tsp garam masala
- 1 tsp fennel seeds
- 1 tsp coriander powder
- ½ tsp turmeric
- 2 tbsp mustard oil
- Salt to taste

Instructions:

1. Heat mustard oil, sauté onions, garlic, and ginger.
2. Add spices, cook for 2 minutes, then stir in tomatoes and yogurt.
3. Add chicken and cook until browned.
4. Simmer for 20 minutes until chicken is tender.
5. Serve with rice or paratha.

Gatte Ki Sabzi

Ingredients:

- 1 cup gram flour (besan)
- 1 onion, finely chopped
- 2 tomatoes, chopped
- 2 cloves garlic, minced
- 1-inch ginger, grated
- 1 tsp cumin seeds
- 1 tsp coriander powder
- 1 tsp garam masala
- ½ tsp turmeric
- 1 tbsp yogurt
- 2 tbsp oil
- Salt to taste

Instructions:

1. Make dough from gram flour, salt, and water, roll into logs, and boil.
2. Slice the boiled dough into pieces.
3. Heat oil, sauté cumin seeds, onions, garlic, and ginger.
4. Add tomatoes, yogurt, and spices, cook for 5 minutes.
5. Add gatte pieces and cook for 15 minutes. Serve with roti.

Tomato Curry (Tamatar Ka Salan)

Ingredients:

- 4 ripe tomatoes, chopped
- 1 onion, finely chopped
- 2 cloves garlic, minced
- 1-inch ginger, grated
- 1 tsp cumin seeds
- 1 tsp coriander powder
- 1 tsp garam masala
- ½ tsp turmeric
- 1 tsp red chili powder
- 2 tbsp oil
- Salt to taste

Instructions:

1. Heat oil, sauté cumin seeds, onions, garlic, and ginger.
2. Add tomatoes and cook for 5 minutes.
3. Stir in spices and cook for another 10 minutes.
4. Simmer until the curry thickens and serve with rice or roti.

Drumstick Curry

Ingredients:

- 2 drumsticks, cut into pieces
- 1 onion, chopped
- 2 tomatoes, chopped
- 2 cloves garlic, minced
- 1-inch ginger, grated
- 1 tsp cumin seeds
- 1 tsp coriander powder
- 1 tsp turmeric
- 1 tsp garam masala
- 1 cup coconut milk
- 2 tbsp oil
- Salt to taste

Instructions:

1. Heat oil, sauté onions, garlic, and ginger.
2. Add tomatoes and spices, cook for 5 minutes.
3. Add drumstick pieces and cook for 10 minutes.
4. Pour in coconut milk, simmer for 15 minutes.
5. Serve with rice.

Black Chana Curry

Ingredients:

- 1 cup black chickpeas (black chana), soaked overnight
- 1 onion, chopped
- 2 tomatoes, chopped
- 2 cloves garlic, minced
- 1-inch ginger, grated
- 1 tsp cumin seeds
- 1 tsp coriander powder
- 1 tsp garam masala
- ½ tsp turmeric
- 1 tsp red chili powder
- 2 tbsp oil
- Salt to taste

Instructions:

1. Cook soaked black chana with water and salt until tender.
2. Heat oil, sauté cumin seeds, onions, garlic, and ginger.
3. Stir in tomatoes and spices, cook for 5 minutes.
4. Add cooked chickpeas and simmer for 10 minutes.
5. Serve with rice or roti.

Achari Chicken

Ingredients:

- 500g chicken, cut into pieces
- 1 onion, finely chopped
- 2 tomatoes, chopped
- 2 cloves garlic, minced
- 1-inch ginger, grated
- 1 tbsp mustard seeds
- 1 tsp fennel seeds
- 1 tsp cumin seeds
- 1 tsp coriander powder
- 1 tsp garam masala
- 1 tbsp yogurt
- 2 tbsp oil
- Salt to taste

Instructions:

1. Heat oil, sauté mustard seeds, fennel, cumin, and onions.
2. Add garlic, ginger, tomatoes, and cook for 5 minutes.
3. Stir in spices and yogurt, then add chicken and cook until browned.
4. Simmer for 20 minutes and serve with naan or rice.

Karela (Bitter Gourd) Curry

Ingredients:

- 2 bitter gourds (karela), sliced
- 1 onion, chopped
- 2 tomatoes, chopped
- 2 cloves garlic, minced
- 1-inch ginger, grated
- 1 tsp cumin seeds
- ½ tsp turmeric
- 1 tsp coriander powder
- 1 tsp red chili powder
- 2 tbsp oil
- Salt to taste

Instructions:

1. Sauté sliced karela in oil until slightly crispy. Remove and set aside.
2. In the same pan, sauté onions, garlic, ginger, and spices.
3. Add tomatoes, cook for 5 minutes, then add karela back.
4. Cook for 10 minutes and serve with roti.

Sambar

Ingredients:

- 1 cup toor dal (yellow lentils)
- 1 onion, chopped
- 2 tomatoes, chopped
- 1 carrot, chopped
- 1 potato, chopped
- 1 drumstick, chopped
- 1 tbsp sambar powder
- ½ tsp turmeric
- 1 tsp mustard seeds
- 2 cloves garlic, minced
- 2 tbsp tamarind pulp
- 2 tbsp oil
- Salt to taste

Instructions:

1. Cook toor dal with turmeric and salt until soft.
2. Heat oil, sauté mustard seeds, onions, garlic, and vegetables.
3. Add tomatoes, cook for 5 minutes, then add cooked dal and tamarind pulp.
4. Stir in sambar powder and simmer for 15 minutes.
5. Serve with rice or idli.

www.ingramcontent.com/pod-product-compliance
Lightning Source LLC
LaVergne TN
LVHW081329060526
838201LV00055B/2539